© Copyright 2020

This document is geared towards providing exact and reliable information with regards to the topic and issue covered. The publication is sold with the idea that the publisher is not required to render accounting, officially permitted,

or otherwise, qualified services.

If advice is necessary, legal or professional, a practised individual

in the profession should be ordered.
From a Declaration of Principles which was accepted and approved equally by a Committee of the American Bar Association and a Committee
of Publishers and Associations.

In no way is it legal to reproduce, duplicate, or transmit any part of this document in either electronic means or in printed format. Recording of this publication is strictly prohibited and any storage of this document is not allowed unless with written permission from the publisher. All rights reserved.

The information provided herein is stated to be truthful and consistent, in that any liability, in terms of inattention or otherwise, by any usage or abuse of any policies, processes, or directions contained within is the solitary and utter responsibility of the recipient reader.

Under no circumstances will any legal responsibility or blame be held against the publisher for any reparation, damages, or monetary loss due to the information herein, either directly or indirectly.

Respective authors own all copyrights not held by the publisher.

The information herein is offered for informational purposes solely, and is universal as so. The presentation of the information is without contract or any type of guarantee assurance.

The trademarks that are used are without any consent, and the publication of the trademark is without permission or backing by the trademark owner.
All trademarks and brands within this book are for clarifying purposes only and are owned by the owners themselves, not affiliated with this document.

Harry Potter
COLORING BOOK

CPSIA information can be obtained
at www.ICGtesting.com
Printed in the USA
BVHW011056150820
586517BV00016B/938